Historic American
LIGHTHOUSES

Historic American
LIGHTHOUSES

BARNES
& NOBLE
BOOKS
NEW YORK

This edition published by Barnes & Noble, Inc.,
by arrangement with becker&mayer!

Copyright © 2003 by becker&mayer!, Ltd.

Historic American Lighthouses is produced
by becker&mayer!, Ltd., Bellevue, Washington
www.beckermayer.com

Editorial: Ben Raker
Design: Todd Bates
Research: Shayna Ian
Production coordination: Cindy Lashley
Project management: Sheila Kamuda

With contributions from Ray Jones and Bruce Roberts.

Printed in China.

ISBN 0-7607-4856-X

Library of Congress Cataloging-in-Publication data is available.

M 10 9 8 7 6 5 4 3 2 1

Contents

Standing guard at the border between land and sea, lighthouses are by nature historical structures. They keep watch over crowded harbors, heavily traveled maritime channels, deadly shoals, and killer reefs, marking not just the passing of ships but the passage of time itself. Strategically located near important landfalls or key port cities, they have witnessed turbulence and tranquility, war and peace, and the comings and goings of commercial, cultural, and political change—the very tides of history.

Often the ages of lighthouses can be measured in generations, if not centuries. Of course, being manmade structures, navigational towers do not last forever, and a large number of them have ended their days in a tumbled heap on a beach or at the base of some weathered cliff. More than a few have fallen victim to shot and shell in wartime, to chance fires, to sudden storms, or to wrecking cranes.

Fortunately, hundreds of fine old lighthouses still dot America's shores. Featured in this book are several of the most historic of these buildings. For instance, the venerable towers at Portland Head (discussed in Chapter One) in Maine, and Cape Hatteras (Chapter Two) in North Carolina, are almost as old as the nation they serve. Florida's red brick Ponce de Leon Inlet Light tower (Chapter Three) was completed in 1887 at a time when the Sunshine State had far more alligators than people. The Old Point Loma Lighthouse (Chapter Four) near San Diego dates to 1856, just a few years after the California Gold Rush.

Bodie Island Light,
North Carolina
Following pages:
Portland Head Light, Maine

The spectacular Heceta Head Lighthouse (Chapter Five) has been warning ships away from Oregon's rugged central coast since the 1880s. Minnesota's Split Rock Lighthouse (Chapter Six) near the western end of mighty Lake Superior was built by immigrant laborers in 1910, several years before the doughboys set sail for Europe and the battlefields of World War I.

Each of these revered coastal towers has a dramatic story to tell—an Indian attack on an isolated Florida light station, a shipwreck that literally crashed the Christmas Eve celebration of a keeper and his family, and disasters such as the sinking of the legendary lake freighter *Edmund Fitzgerald*. As these stories and others unfold on the pages that follow, you'll see how the lighthouses pictured in this book relate to American history, and you'll learn why each of them represents an important step in the development of navigational technology and the improvement of maritime safety.

Lighthouses are historical treasures because they remind us of a maritime heritage that we had best never forget. However, they are very unlike museum displays or cold marble monuments that celebrate history in a passive way. Lighthouses still have a job to do. Even though radar and computerized shipboard electronics have made them less important to navigation than once was the case, lighthouse beacons continue to guide mariners. They remain a vital national resource, for America has always been and will remain a seafaring nation, relying on lighthouses—in one form or another—to guide our ships safely home.

Heceta Head Light, Oregon

Split Rock Light, Minnesota

Old Point Loma Light, California

CHAPTER ONE

Northeastern Lights
and the Revolutionary Era

A few miles from the busy commercial harbor at Portland, Maine, a craggy headland pushes eastward into the Atlantic. This rocky, almost barren place is home to one of the most beautiful and beloved structures in all America—the Portland Head Lighthouse. Its spectacular setting, bold architecture, and two centuries of fascinating history attract a steady stream of camera-toting visitors, but while it serves as both a historical monument and an inspiration to artists and photographers, it continues to guide vessels safely into port. It remains a hard-working aid to navigation.

The light station at Portland Head was established in 1791, only two years after the adoption of the United States Constitution. President George Washington himself ordered construction of the rough-stone Portland Head tower, the first major project undertaken by the fledgling U.S. federal government. Although never a seaman himself, Washington understood that America could not grow and prosper without access to sea trade. He recognized that America lacked an adequate system of navigational markers to point the way to ports and warn vessels away from rocks, reefs, and other dangerous obstacles. Lighthouses were needed to stimulate commerce and

Portland Head Light, Maine
Following pages: Portland
Head Light, Maine

make the nation's shores as safe as possible for mariners. So, urged on by the president, Congress made passage of a lighthouse bill one of its very first official acts. This measure placed responsibility for existing lighthouses in federal hands and authorized construction of new ones.

By the time lighthouses became a matter of federal concern, the Commonwealth of Massachusetts had already started building a light tower on Portland Head. Strapped with debts left over from the Revolutionary War, however, Massachusetts soon ran out of money, and the project ground to a halt. To get it moving again, Washington sent Secretary of the Treasury Alexander Hamilton to Congress with a request for funding. Congress replied with a stingy appropriation of $1,500—barely enough to complete the tower. To save money on materials, laborers gathered stones from nearby fields and hauled them to the construction site with the help of oxen. Despite the short funding and delays caused by gales and heavy snows, the tower stood ready for duty by January of 1791, and Joseph Greenleaf, the first Portland Head keeper, was able to light the station's lamps. From that time forward, vessels entering Portland Harbor at night had a light to guide them.

> Lighthouses were needed to stimulate commerce and make the nation's shores as safe as possible for mariners. So, urged on by the president, Congress made passage of a lighthouse bill one of its very first official acts.

Nobska Point Light,
Massachusetts

Unfortunately, during its early decades, the Portland Head Light offered only limited assistance to mariners,

especially those more than a few miles from shore. Fog frequently obscured the station's relatively weak beacon, and the height of its tower—only about eighty feet—restricted the range of the light. Eventually, maritime authorities had the tower raised to over a hundred feet and fitted it with a Fresnel lens, regarded during the nineteenth century as the very latest in lighthouse optical technology.

The added height and powerful new lens gave the beacon a substantial range of up to twenty miles. Mariners could now count on the Portland Head Light for guidance even while their vessels were still far out at sea. It is impossible to say how many ships and lives have been saved by this light during its more than two hundred years of service, but the numbers are significant.

Despite the station's much-improved beacon, however, ships continued to be lost in the dangerous waters off Portland Head. One notable wreck, that of the three-masted sailing ship *Annie Maguire,* occurred in the very shadow of the light tower. It happened in the midst of a blizzard on December 24, 1888, just as keeper Joshua Strout and his family were about to enjoy their Christmas Eve festivities. Alarmed by a thunderous crash, Strout ran outside to discover a sizeable wooden freighter grounded on the rocks only a few yards from the door of the lighthouse. Despite the high winds and pounding surf, the *Maguire's* freezing crew of fifteen made it safely ashore, where they shared a hot holiday meal with the Strouts.

New London Harbor
Light, Connecticut
Following pages:
Pemaquid Point
Light, Maine

Even though the Portland Head Lighthouse and its beacon are less vital to maritime safety than once was the case, its light continues to shine each night, keeping alive a tradition of service reaching back more than two centuries. Hundreds of other active light stations still share in that tradition. So do many inactive lighthouses that now serve as museums or as key attractions of historic parks and monuments—reminders of the nation's rich lighthouse heritage.

The American lighthouse story had its beginnings in the eighteenth century. When federal authorities took charge of America's system of navigational markers, that system included only a handful of coastal lights, most of them established during colonial times. Prominent among the light stations placed in service by the original thirteen colonies were the Brant Point (established in 1746), Cape Ann (1768), and Plymouth (1771) Lights, all in Massachusetts, Portsmouth Light (1771) in New Hampshire, Beavertail Light (1749) in Rhode Island, New London Light (1760) in Connecticut, Sandy Hook Light (1764) in New Jersey, Cape Henlopen Light (1765) in Delaware, and Charleston Light (1767) in South Carolina. However, the granddaddy of all these early beacons was the one shining from Little Brewster Island at the entrance to Boston Harbor.

[T]he Boston Light Station had served mariners for more than half a century by the time Paul Revere made his famous ride in 1775.

Established by the colony of Massachusetts in 1716, the Boston Light Station had served mariners for more than half a century by the time Paul Revere made his famous

Boston Harbor Light, Massachusetts

Cape Neddick Light, Maine

Minots Ledge Light, Massachusetts

ride in 1775. To meet the costs of maintaining the light-house, colonial officials collected a duty of one penny for each ton of shipping that entered the harbor. The funds thus raised were used to pay a number of expenses, including the keeper's salary, which was initially set at a mere fifty British pounds per year. The first keeper to draw this modest salary was a hapless man named George Worthylake, who drowned after less than two years on the job. The station was to have several dozen other keepers, however, and most of them proved much luckier than Worthylake.

Solidly built with stone, the original Boston tower stood for sixty years. It might still stand today had the British not exploded it with barrels of gunpowder as they retreated from Boston during the Revolutionary War. Rebuilt in 1783, the Boston Lighthouse remains in service, a durable relic of early American times.

Although Boston was the site of America's first light station, its 1783 tower is not the nation's oldest. That honor goes to an eighty-five-foot, octagonal stone structure on New Jersey's Sandy Hook near the entrance to New York's Lower Bay. Completed in 1764, the tower was built not by New Jersey, but rather by business-minded New Yorkers who hoped to attract more commerce to the docks of New York City. Like the Boston Lighthouse, the Sandy Hook Light Station played a role in the Revolutionary War, but with less disastrous results for the old colonial tower. It survived considerable abuse by the British as well as repeated attacks by Continental soldiers who hoped to prevent the redcoats from using it to guide their warships into the Hudson River.

Sandy Hook Light,
New Jersey

Washington and other early American leaders understood only too well that the Boston Light, the Sandy Hook Light, and the dozen or so other lighthouses that marked America's shores before 1790 were far too few in number to meet the nation's navigational needs. They envisioned a chain of navigational lights extending along the entire length of the U.S. shoreline. These beacons would overlap so that vessels moving along the coast always had a light to guide them.

Construction of the many new towers required to make the chain a reality began in earnest during the 1790s. Having completed the Portland Head Lighthouse in 1791, the government moved on to establish important light stations at Cape Henry (1791) in Virginia, Tybee Island (1791) in Georgia, Seguin Island (1795) in Maine, Montauk Point (1797) in New York, Gay Head (1799) on Martha's Vineyard in Massachusetts, Cape Hatteras (1803) in North Carolina, and scores of other strategic locations.

The system of navigational lights created in colonial times and expanded by the U.S. federal government eventually became the best and most extensive in the world. As the nation grew, so did its Lighthouse Service. In time, its beacons marked not just the nation's eastern shores, but the coasts of Florida and the states along the Gulf of Mexico, the rugged cliffs of California and the Pacific Northwest, and the shores of the Great Lakes, whose waters carried maritime commerce to the very heart of the North American continent.

Montauk Point Light,
New York

Seguin Island Light, Maine

Bass Harbor Head Light, Maine

CHAPTER TWO

Mid-Atlantic Lights and the Move at Cape Hatteras

*T*he most famous lighthouse in the world is almost certainly the grand old brick tower that anchors the southeastern end of North Carolina's Hatteras Island. Considered by many the quintessential American lighthouse, the spiral-striped tower has been seen on television and in magazine photographs so many times in recent years that it is nearly impossible to envision a coastal scene without including in it a view of the Cape Hatteras Lighthouse. Ironically, the giant, 193-foot structure earned all this attention by nearly being swept into the Atlantic Ocean.

The natural forces that made the tower vulnerable—and almost destroyed it—are the very same ones that caused the Cape Hatteras Lighthouse to be built in the first place. Two rivers of seawater—the Gulf Stream and the Labrador Current—collide with one another close to the Cape Hatteras shore, causing riptides that race up and down the North Carolina coast. Constantly scouring beaches and reshaping the long line of barrier islands known as the Outer Banks, these currents build shoals and shallows and cause vessels to careen dangerously off course.

Cape Hatteras Light, North Carolina, after relocation

Seamen unfamiliar with these waters should—and usually do—keep their distance, but even knowledgeable skippers can make fatal errors off the Outer Banks. In fact, so many vessels have been lost on or near these shores that the area is widely known as the "Graveyard of the Atlantic."

Throughout the nineteenth century, U.S. maritime authorities struggled to mark the Outer Banks and provide mariners with adequate warning. In addition to the Cape Hatteras Lighthouse, built during the administration of President Thomas Jefferson, tall towers were erected at Cape Lookout in 1812, Bodie Island in 1847, and Currituck Beach in 1875. These light stations were rebuilt or improved at various times as the need arose and as congressional appropriations became available.

For instance, the Bodie Island Lighthouse, about forty miles north of Cape Hatteras, was rebuilt no fewer than three times. It started out as a poorly constructed, fifty-four-foot pile of bricks stacked on top of a foundation so unstable that the structure had to be torn down and replaced after only a few years of service. A second Bodie Island tower, completed in 1859, was blown up by Confederate raiders during the Civil War. The existing tower with its bold black-and-white bands dates to 1872.

At about the time work began on the third Bodie Island tower—the same one that marks the island

Cape Lookout Light,
North Carolina
Following pages: Bodie
Island Light, North Carolina

today—laborers were putting the finishing touches on a completely rebuilt Cape Hatteras Lighthouse. The crucial Cape Hatteras beacon, thought by many to be the most important navigational marker in America, had long been considered inadequate by mariners. More than a few ships had run aground on nearby Diamond Shoals while their captains watched in vain for the light. One of the vessels lost on the shoals was the Civil War ironclad *Monitor*. Only a few months after her famous but inconclusive slugfest with the Confederate warship *Virginia* in 1862, the *Monitor* ran into a gale and foundered about twelve miles from Cape Hatteras.

The loss of the *Monitor* and so many other vessels off the Outer Banks spurred federal maritime officials to act, and following the war, work began on a new and much taller Cape Hatteras tower. Completed in 1870, it soared more than 190 feet above the nearly featureless island. Stretching out over the ocean from this considerable elevation, the powerful Cape Hatteras beacon could now reach sailors on vessels more than twenty miles away.

The natural forces that made the tower vulnerable—and almost destroyed it—are the very same ones that caused the Cape Hatteras Lighthouse to be built in the first place.

Once the new Cape Hatteras Lighthouse began operation, the old tower was blown up and left lying on the beach, a jumble of shattered bricks and mortar awash in the tides. Not many years ago experts were predicting a similar unhappy fate for the present-day Cape

Cape Hatteras Light, North Carolina, before relocation

Hatteras Lighthouse. This time the threat was not an intentionally set explosion, but rather the irresistible advance of the Atlantic. Beach erosion along the Outer Banks is such that no structure here can be considered permanent. A dozen feet or more of beachfront property may be carried away by a single ocean storm so that homes and businesses built too close to the tides are always at risk.

Originally, the Cape Hatteras Lighthouse stood nearly half a mile from the ocean, but the Atlantic eventually whittled this down to less than a hundred yards. Several times since 1870 the rampaging tides have advanced almost to within reach of the tower's vulnerable foundation only to retreat again to a seemingly safe distance. Then, during the waning years of the twentieth century, the Atlantic launched what appeared to be its final attack on the tower. Waves rushed toward it on three sides, and there were many who believed the tower could no longer stand up to a major sea storm. All attempts to hold back the tides by constructing barriers or pumping fresh sand onto the beach seemed destined to fail. As it turned out, the only way to save the lighthouse was to move it.

Managed by the National Park Service and funded by a special $12 million federal appropriation, the relocation took place during the spring of 1999. As one might imagine, moving a 4,800-ton brick tower almost two-thirds as tall as a football field is long, proved a tremendous challenge. Despite its mass, the

Cape Hatteras Light,
North Carolina,
showing path of travel

one-and-a-third-centuries-old building was surprisingly delicate, and preventing it from falling apart during the move was the primary and constant concern of the relocation team.

To protect the tower while moving it, the team employed a combination of space-age technology and engineering principles as old as the lighthouse itself. Having excavated the soil and sand beneath the building, the movers lifted it with hydraulic jacks onto a platform of hefty steel supports. Then shortly after 3:00 p.m. on June 17, 1999, the venerable lighthouse began its journey. Gliding ever so slowly over steel rails lubricated with ordinary hand soap, the tower traveled only a few feet each hour, a pace barely perceptible to the eye.

During the move, the Cape Hatteras Lighthouse became an international celebrity. Reporters and camera crews from across the nation came to Hatteras Island to observe the relocation process. Elementary school classes kept track of the tower's progress, and practically everyone watched the slow-motion spectacle on television news broadcasts. Well-wishers around the world were relieved and delighted when, on the afternoon of July 9, almost exactly twenty-two days after its momentous trek began, the lighthouse safely reached its destination.

As one might imagine, moving a 4,800-ton brick tower almost two-thirds as tall as a football field is long, proved a tremendous challenge.

Cape Hatteras Light, North Carolina, showing steel rails used in relocation

Placed on a solid foundation some sixteen hundred feet inland, the tower now stands far enough from the Atlantic tides to keep it safe for generations to come. Having resumed its task of guiding mariners, the Cape Hatteras Lighthouse now serves not just as a vital aid to navigation but also as an important symbol. The successful relocation of the Cape Hatteras tower has engendered a fresh appreciation of the nation's rich maritime heritage—and not coincidentally, of lighthouses and the need to preserve them. Young people, especially, seem more interested in the preservation of historic structures.

During the move, the Cape Hatteras Lighthouse became an international celebrity.

Tourists now flock to Hatteras Island to see the big tower and learn about its extraordinary rescue. Usually, lighthouse lovers who visit Cape Hatteras also stop in at the Bodie Island Light Station, located on North Carolina Route 12 a few miles south of Nags Head, and at the entrance to the Cape Hatteras National Seashore. The two-story, wooden keeper's residence houses a museum recalling more than 150 years of the station's history. Here visitors may get a sense of what life was like for keepers and their families at this isolated and rather rustic government facility.

Although located well to the north of the popular beach resorts at Nags Head and Kittyhawk in an out-of-the-way corner of the Outer Banks, the Currituck

Cape Hatteras Light, North Carolina, after relocation

Assateague Light, Virginia

Old Cape Henry Light, Virginia

Beach Lighthouse also claims its share of visitors. Most elect to climb the 214 steps to the lantern room at the top of the 162-foot brick tower. There they are rewarded with an unparalleled view of the Atlantic Ocean to the east, the broad sounds to the west, and the narrow strip of sandy barrier islands where so many vessels have ended their days.

Currituck Beach keepers made this same climb several times each evening from 1875, when the station was completed, until 1939, when the Coast Guard automated the light. At Currituck Beach, as elsewhere, a keeper's most important responsibility was to keep the light burning, a duty that required repeated visits to the lofty lantern room. This was especially important during the years before electricity reached the remote station and incandescent bulbs replaced its old-style oil lamps. The latter required frequent refueling, and their wicks had to be kept in perfect trim.

Like Bodie Island and many other historic light stations, the Currituck Beach Lighthouse features an excellent visitors center and museum housed in the former keeper's dwelling, but the station's most remarkable feature is its still-functioning, first-order Fresnel lens. Among the largest of its kind, this huge polished-glass prismatic optic focuses the station's flashing white beacon. Funneled into a concentrated beam by the prisms, the light can

[E]ven knowledgeable skippers can make fatal errors off the Outer Banks. In fact, so many vessels have been lost on or near these shores that the area is widely known as the "Graveyard of the Atlantic."

Currituck Beach Light,
North Carolina

be seen from twenty miles or more out in the Atlantic. The beacon's considerable range enables it to warn mariners long before they approach the dangerous shallows close to shore.

While expensive to maintain, Fresnel lenses such as the one at Currituck Beach perform the task of alerting mariners just as well or better than supposedly more sophisticated modern optics. When they were introduced to American lighthouses during the latter half of the nineteenth century, they were rightly considered a marvel of science. The next chapter includes an ample discussion of these fascinating and beautiful devices.

Bodie Island Light,
North Carolina
Following pages: Drum
Point Light, Maryland

CHAPTER THREE

Florida Lights
and the Fresnel Lens

*L*ikely there is no museum in America more dazzling than the one that stands beside the Ponce de Leon Inlet Lighthouse just south of Daytona Beach, Florida. Several of the buildings that once served as work or storage areas or as housing for the station's keeper and crew are now used for the display of maritime and lighthouse artifacts. One building in particular is special because it contains a fine array of lighthouse optics including a number of sparkling Fresnel lenses.

Early lighthouses were limited by the inefficiency of their beacons. No matter how brightly it burns, a lamp or candle cannot be seen from any considerable distance. This is because the light is diffuse and radiates in all directions, its brightness steadily diminishing in strength as it gets farther from its source. Attempts were made to increase the range of early lighthouse beacons by using carefully shaped mirrors, but these proved of limited usefulness.

Ponce de Leon
Inlet Light, Florida
Following pages: Fresnel
lens of the Point Gratiot
Light, New York

In 1810, a former sea captain named Winslow Lewis introduced a system of high-intensity oil lamps and parabolic reflectors intended to make American navigational

beacons more powerful. Impressed by Lewis's new optical devices, the government paid the old seaman to place them in all U.S. lighthouses. No doubt, the Lewis lamps and reflectors made a difference, but mariners still complained that American lighthouse beacons were not bright enough. Wrecks along the U.S. coast continued at an alarming rate, and a disheartening number of these accidents occurred because pilots and navigators were unable to see the beacons that otherwise might have guided them to safety.

Meanwhile, in Europe, a French scientist and inventor named Augustin Fresnel had made a stunning breakthrough in optical technology. In 1822, Fresnel introduced a lens capable of concentrating light so efficiently that it could be seen over a distance of twenty miles or more. These lenses consisted of an array of highly polished, light-bending glass prisms—sometimes more than a thousand—set in a brass frame. The prisms collected nearly all of the light that fell on them, funneling it into a single, powerful beam. Some Fresnel lenses contained bull's-eyes, which produced a flashing effect when the lens was rotated.

Early lighthouses were limited by the inefficiency of their beacons. No matter how brightly it burns, a lamp or candle cannot be seen from any considerable distance.

Soon French companies began to manufacture and sell the new lenses—often at eye-popping prices. They were produced in a variety of sizes or "orders" ranging from the diminutive sixth-order lenses, which were little

Lantern room of the Currituck Beach Light, North Carolina, showing the inside of its Fresnel lens

more than a foot wide, up to the massive first-order lenses, which could be more than six feet wide and weigh several tons. The larger lenses were particularly expensive; one of these lenses might carry a price tag larger than the cost of building the lighthouse itself.

No doubt, mariners whose ships and lives were saved by bright Fresnel beacons would argue they were worth every penny of their price, but that was not the attitude of tightfisted Washington bureaucrats such as Stephen Pleasonton. A U.S. Treasury auditor who for more than thirty years controlled the monies spent on U.S. navigational aids, Pleasonton favored the cheaper and far less effective Lewis reflectors. Only after Pleasonton lost authority over America's lighthouses during the early 1850s were Fresnel lenses imported in large numbers.

In 1852, Congress placed administration of the nation's coastal markers in the hands of a Lighthouse Board composed of military and civilian engineers. Almost immediately, the board undertook a complete overhaul of the lighthouse system. Rickety towers were torn down and rebuilt, lamps and lanterns (the housings at the tops of lighthouse towers) were standardized and improved, and Fresnel lenses were installed. The new Fresnels proved so effective that many of them remain in use today even though most are more than a century old.

First-order Fresnel lens housed in the Pensacola Light, Florida

Nowhere was the modernizing influence of the Lighthouse Board felt more strongly than in Florida.

Like the North Carolina Outer Banks far to the north, the flat, nearly featureless Florida shoreline had a reputation for chewing up ships. Especially menacing were the Keys, a chain of small islands stretching more than a hundred miles southwestward from Cape Florida. Whole fleets had been ruined by the Keys' deadly coral reefs, but the Lighthouse Board knew the entire Florida coast was dangerous. Marking it properly required navigational beacons with a long reach, able to warn mariners while they were still at a safe distance from the shore.

> [I]n Florida, the
> Lighthouse Board
> ordered construction of
> some of the nation's
> tallest light towers and
> equipped them with the
> best optics available

The exceptional power made possible by Fresnel's light-concentrating technology meant that the range of a lighthouse beacon need only be limited by the elevation of its focal plane. So, in Florida, the Lighthouse Board ordered construction of some of the nation's tallest light towers and equipped them with the best optics available—imported Fresnel lenses. For instance, first-order Fresnels were placed in the 150-foot conical brick tower at Pensacola (completed in 1859), the 125-foot brick tower at Jupiter Inlet (1860), the 145-foot brick-lined metal tower at Cape Canaveral (1868), the 165-foot brick tower at St. Augustine (1874), and the 168-foot red-brick tower at Ponce de Leon Inlet (1887). All these light stations remain in use, and those at Pensacola, St. Augustine, and Jupiter Inlet still employ their enormous first-order lenses.

Jupiter Inlet Light, Florida

Tall towers and powerful beacons were also needed in the Florida Keys, but here Lighthouse Board crews had to build them in open water. Furthermore, these structures had to be extremely durable and able to withstand constant exposure to salt water as well as the annual onslaught of tropical storms. The brick, stone, or wooden towers erected elsewhere would never last in such an inhospitable environment, so a fresh approach was required.

To devise one, the Board turned to young, innovative engineers the likes of George Meade. A West Point graduate and U.S. Army engineer, Meade would later write his name into history books as the Civil War general who led Union forces to victory at Gettysburg. Working for the Lighthouse Board in the Florida Keys during the 1850s, however, the threats he confronted were gales and high tides rather than Confederate cannon fire and musketry.

The new Fresnels [installed in the 1850s] proved so effective that many of them remain in use today even though most are more than a century old.

Meade believed that a new breed of all-metal tower could survive the harsh open-ocean environment and stand up to the hurricanes that swept over the Keys nearly every year. Consisting of heavily braced cast-iron legs anchored securely to the sea floor by piles, these skeletal structures allowed high waves and whistling, gale-force winds to pass harmlessly through their open walls. Meade designed or helped build several lighthouses of this type in the Keys. Perhaps the

Top of the St. Augustine Light, Florida
Following pages:
Fresnel lens shown at the museum at the Ponce de Leon Inlet Light, Florida

best known of Meade's lighthouses was the one he built on Sand Key about seven miles south of Key West. Originally, a brick lighthouse had marked Sand Key, but in 1848 a hurricane swept it away along with the keeper and three visitors who happened to be at the station when the storm struck. Stung by this tragedy, the Lighthouse Board was determined to replace the demolished lighthouse with a tower that could survive any storm. Completed by Meade in 1853, the new tower stood on a forest of iron legs. Its keeper's dwelling was positioned between the legs and elevated to protect it from waves. The lantern room at the top of 105-foot Sand Key tower once held a sparkling first-order Fresnel lens. The Fresnel lens and keeper's dwelling were removed years ago, but the station, now equipped with a modern optic, remains in service to this day.

> [T]he flat, nearly featureless Florida shoreline had a reputation for chewing up ships. Especially menacing were the Keys, a chain of small islands stretching more than a hundred miles southwestward from Cape Florida.

Meade also built lighthouses on the mainland, among the last of them the conical brick tower at Jupiter Inlet. Completed in 1860, only about a year before the opening shots of the Civil War, the project gave rise to one of history's more poignant ironies. Robert E. Lee surveyed the site for this station, which George Meade built, the two men cooperating in an endeavor intended mainly to save human life. Later Lee and Meade would lead the opposing armies at Gettysburg, where thousands of Americans were slain.

Key West Light, Florida

Alligator Reef Light, Florida

Sand Key Light, Florida

The Civil War had been over for more than twenty years by the time the finishing touches were put on the Ponce de Leon Inlet Lighthouse south of Daytona in 1887. An earlier light tower had been built here during the 1830s, but before its lamps could be installed, the tower was damaged beyond repair in a raid by Seminole Indians. Half a century passed before the government tried again to mark the inlet with a major lighthouse, but this time the attempt succeeded. Although its first-order lens has been replaced by an automated modern optic, the station still guides mariners along what was once an especially dark and dangerous stretch of east Florida coast. The old Fresnel lens is now on display at the adjacent museum along with a truly worthy array of other lighthouse optics and artifacts.

Ponce de Leon
Inlet Light, Florida

St. Augustine Light, Florida

Cape St. George Light, Florida

CHAPTER FOUR

California and the First Pacific Lights

*W*hen the United States acquired Florida from the Spanish in 1821, federal maritime authorities shouldered the daunting responsibility of marking its lengthy Atlantic and Gulf coasts with adequate navigational lights. The task was still far from complete three decades later when California came under the U.S. flag, adding another eight hundred miles to the nation's coastline. With countless thousands of gold rush prospectors and land-hungry settlers heading west, many of them by ship, lighthouse officials recognized that the navigational needs of the Pacific Coast could no longer be ignored. By 1850, when California entered the Union, not one government lighthouse stood between San Diego and the settlements along Puget Sound nearly two thousand miles to the north, but that was about to change.

Not long after it was established by Congress in 1852, the Lighthouse Board launched an ambitious construction program in the west. Contractors were hired to build major lighthouses at strategic Pacific Coast locations such as Alcatraz Island (completed in 1854) in San Francisco Bay, Cape Disappointment (1856) at

Stairwell inside the Point Arena Light, California
Following pages: Alcatraz Island Light, California

the mouth of the Columbia River, and Cape Flattery (1857) near the entrance to the Strait of Juan de Fuca. As a cost-saving measure, the government placed construction of the first eight of these western towers in the hands of a single talented contractor, a veteran engineer named Francis Gibbons.

Having built lighthouses on the Outer Banks and elsewhere in the east, Gibbons brought a wealth of experience with him to California. He also brought the *Oriole,* a sailing ship loaded with special equipment and supplies, which made the trip to California by way of a twelve-thousand-mile journey around the tip of South America. The *Oriole,* with its load of materials, docked at San Francisco late in the fall of 1852, and Gibbons immediately started work on the Alcatraz Island Lighthouse.

The government had saddled Gibbons with a mammoth undertaking—the construction of eight lighthouses on isolated sites scattered along the coast from the Columbia River to San Diego—but he organized the project with machine-like efficiency. As soon as the foundation at Alcatraz Island had been laid, the crew responsible for that part of the process moved on to lay a second foundation elsewhere, then a third, a fourth, and so on. Other crews were responsible for erecting dwelling and tower walls, putting on roofs, and finishing interiors. Working in stages, Gibbons and his crews had four lighthouses standing within ten months. Then calamity brought work to a standstill.

Cape Disappointment
Light, Washington

The Pacific coast presents ships and sailors with many hazards, but the most dangerous of these hazards is located several hundred miles north of San Francisco at the mouth of the Columbia River. Here the rush of fresh river water into the Pacific has built up a formidable bar, and mariners entering the Columbia have no choice but to cross it and hope they can avoid running aground. The hulls of countless vessels have been shattered in the bar's wave-swept shallows. Ironically, the Cape Disappointment Lighthouse was intended to guide ships safely past this obstacle, but of course, its beacon was not yet shining in August of 1853 when the *Oriole* arrived off the cape with her load of construction materials.

Gibbons meant to begin work on the lighthouse as soon as the *Oriole* had put ashore his supplies, but the supplies never reached him. With no light to show the way, the vessel's master blundered into the bar's treacherous shallows, and the *Oriole* was soon smashed to bits by breakers. No lives were lost, but the freighter's vital cargo was swallowed up by the Pacific.

This disaster pushed Gibbons's company, a partnership with eastern businessman Francis Kelley, to the brink of financial ruin. Even so, the dauntless builder forged ahead. Somehow he raised the money to outfit

By 1850, when California entered the Union, not one government lighthouse stood between San Diego and the settlements along Puget Sound nearly two thousand miles to the north, but that was about to change.

Cape Flattery Light, Washington

81

another ship, and soon, the good work of lighting the nation's western shores was once more underway. By the end of August 1854, Gibbons's crews had completed the Point Loma Lighthouse near San Diego, the last of the eight lighthouses he had agreed to build.

Like most of Gibbons's other lighthouses, however, the Point Loma Light Station was not yet ready for duty. The Alcatraz Island Lighthouse had received its third-order lens and was already guiding ships through San Francisco Bay, but none of the other Gibbons light stations were functional. Sent by sailing ship from France, the all-important Fresnel lenses that were needed to focus the beacons had not yet arrived.

The mammoth first-order lens the government had purchased for Point Loma turned up late in 1855. Much to the chagrin of all concerned, the big lens— more than six feet in diameter—would not fit into the narrow tower Gibbons's crews had built. The same proved to be the case with most of the other towers— they were too small for the lenses that had been ordered for them. Gibbons was forced to renovate several of the towers and completely rebuild others. Having already suffered a huge financial setback with the loss of the *Oriole*, Gibbons abandoned any remaining hope of turning a profit on the project.

Perhaps taking pity on the hapless Gibbons, lighthouse officials decided against having him rebuild the tower at Point Loma. Instead of a first-order Fresnel,

they equipped the station with a smaller and somewhat less powerful third-order lens. This proved of little consequence to the beacon's usefulness since the Point Loma station stood at an elevation of over four hundred feet. From that impressive height, the station's third-order beacon was powerful enough to reach vessels far out at sea. In fact, mariners occasionally reported seeing it from as much as forty miles offshore.

The Point Loma tower itself was only forty-six feet tall. It rose through the roof of a modest, one-and-a-half-story keeper's residence built in Cape Cod style. Several of Gibbons's lighthouses followed the same general plan, that of a small stone dwelling surrounding a relatively short but serviceable tower. This allowed the keeper to work, eat, and sleep in the same building—a practical, if not particularly comfortable, arrangement.

Francis Gibbons built his lighthouses to last, and several of them still stand today, one and a half centuries after they were completed. The Old Point Loma Lighthouse can be counted among these sturdy survivors, a fact that could be viewed as a minor miracle. The building functioned as an active aid to navigation for only thirty-six years and has not served mariners since 1891. As it turned out, the station's considerable elevation proved more hindrance than help. Low-lying clouds and fog often obscured the light so that seamen were least likely to see it at the very times they needed it most. Eventually, the

New Point Loma Light, California

87

Lighthouse Board had a new lighthouse built down closer to the ocean.

After the New Point Loma Lighthouse—a steel-skeleton tower with adjacent two-story residence—was completed in 1891, the elder structure fell into disuse and decay. Over the years several plans to demolish it were considered and then shelved. Finally, in 1933, the historic structure came under the wing of the Cabrillo National Monument, which repaired and refurbished it for use as a museum.

> Francis Gibbons built his lighthouses to last, and several of them still stand today, one and a half centuries after they were completed.

Another of Gibbons's lighthouses, the one he built on Alcatraz Island in 1853, was not so lucky. A building very much like the one atop the Point Loma cliffs, it consisted of a solidly constructed masonry residence with a central tower. Its bright light guided ships for more than fifty years, right up until 1906 when the great San Francisco earthquake all but leveled the lighthouse. By 1909 a reinforced concrete tower had taken the place of the nineteenth-century original.

Beginning in the 1930s, Alcatraz Island became a very rough neighborhood, the home of a maximum-security federal prison for tough guys like Al Capone. Today, the gangsters are gone, but the shell of their unhappy iron and concrete home attracts plenty of curious visitors. Most of the tourists who take the

Pigeon Point Light,
California

ferry to Alcatraz also want to see the lighthouse, which has become one of the most widely recognized symbols of the City by the Bay.

For anyone who loves lighthouses and the history they represent, San Francisco is a Mecca. Within little more than two hours' drive from the bustle of Fisherman's Wharf and Chinatown can be found an astounding array of historic navigational stations. Some surely must be counted among the most beautiful lighthouses in America. For instance, only a few miles from downtown, the lovely Point Bonita Lighthouse marks the seaward approaches to the Golden Gate Strait. Its spectacular setting and attractive wooden access bridge make it one of the most picturesque light stations anywhere, but it has plenty of history to offer as well.

During the gold rush, ships slammed into Point Bonita with alarming regularity. The original, 1855 Point Bonita Lighthouse—one of Gibbons's Cape-style structures—was built too far up on the cliffs to provide an effective warning, especially when fog cloaked the bay. A second lighthouse, completed in 1877, was built closer to the water and was able to handle its task of guiding vessels safely through the strait with considerably more efficiency. Even so, ships continued to founder on the point. Keeper John Brown, who served at Point Bonita for nearly twenty years during the late nineteenth century, made a habit of rescuing shipwrecked sailors. During his years at the station, he pulled more than forty seamen out of the surf.

Point Vincent Light, California
Following pages: Point Bonita Light, California

To the north of San Francisco the rocky Point Reyes Peninsula juts more than ten miles out into the Pacific. Seamen encountering this deadly barrier in a fog— and it is one of the foggiest places in the world—may not live to see the skies clear. To warn them of their peril, a powerful foghorn and light were placed on Point Reyes in 1870. The iron-plated, sixteen-sided tower built more than 130 years ago still clings to the rocks at the far end of the point. Although no longer in use, its nearly priceless first-order Fresnel lens remains in the tower to fascinate and delight visitors to Point Reyes National Seashore.

On the Monterey Peninsula about two hours south of San Francisco, the Point Pinos Lighthouse graces a municipal golf course often more alive with deer and sea gulls than with golfers. Yet another Cape-style structure built by Gibbons during the 1850s, this is California's oldest operating lighthouse. For many years, the Point Pinos Station had a female keeper, a former San Francisco socialite named Emily Fish. It is said that she often entertained sea captains and dignitaries in high style at the keeper's residence.

Point Reyes Light,
California

CHAPTER FIVE

Northwest Lights—
Beacons of a Rugged Coast

*P*erched on the side of an Oregon cliff more than two hundred feet above the Pacific, the Heceta Head Lighthouse flashes its bright signal all night and every night just as it has for more than a century. Its message for mariners is a simple one: "Keep your distance." Wise captains will heed the warning, for the mountain range that meets the Pacific at Heceta Head does not stop at water's edge. Instead, it continues westward into the ocean, creating a deadly menace to ships and sailors. Some peaks rise from the ocean floor to form craggy offshore islands, while others do not break the surface at all, but rather, lurk just below the waves waiting to rip the bottom out of a passing ship. Over the years, more than a few mariners have paid with their lives for straying into this trap.

These hazards were recognized as early as 1755 when Spanish explorer Don Bruno de Heceta noted them on his charts and gave the place a name—his own. Even so, Heceta Head did not receive a major navigational beacon until 1894, long after many lesser coastal threats had been marked. Because of its isolation and rugged terrain, U.S. maritime officials thought building a lighthouse here impractical, if not impossible.

Heceta Head Light,
Oregon

However, a sharp increase in shipping—and ship-wrecks—during the final decades of the nineteenth century convinced them to give it a try.

Undertaken during the early 1890s, construction of the Heceta Head Light Station proved even harder than Lighthouse Board engineers had expected. Materials had to be shipped in from distant ports, brought ashore at a landing on the nearby Suislaw River, and then hauled up the cliffs by mules. It took more than two years and no less than $180,000—a stupendous sum at the time—to complete the fifty-six-foot brick tower, two-story keeper's residence, and fog signal building.

Despite its hefty price, the Heceta Head Lighthouse turned out to be a bargain, a testament to the high quality of nineteenth century workmanship and navigational technology. After more than a century of punishment by fierce Pacific storms, the station remains in operation, its brick walls as sturdy today as when their last bricks were laid in 1894. The station's original first-order Fresnel lens still focuses its light, which can reach ships more than twenty miles away—so-called modern optics could do no better. During a service career now well into its second century, the Heceta Head beacon and fog signal have saved uncounted ships and lives at a cost to American taxpayers (amortized over 110 years) amounting to less than five dollars per day.

> Wise captains will heed the warning, for the mountain range that meets the Pacific at Heceta Head does not stop at water's edge.

Heceta Head Light, Oregon
Following pages:
Heceta Head Light, Oregon, at sunset

At many points along the coast of the Pacific Northwest, lighthouse engineers and construction crews grappled with difficulties equal to or exceeding those facing them at Heceta Head. Probably the greatest challenge they ever confronted came at Tillamook Rock, a barren hunk of basalt rising like a fist from the Pacific a mile or so off the north coast of Oregon. Put ashore on the rock in October 1879, workers and their supervisors had to live out in the open, bracing themselves against the cold and rain and taking whatever shelter they could during storms. Having blasted a foundation from the solid basalt with dynamite, they painstakingly erected a fortress-like barracks for themselves and then started work on the lighthouse.

Their task was a difficult and wearying one. Materials could only be delivered on those rare days when the ocean was calm. When gales blew in off the Pacific, workers were cut off from all outside contact, and during prolonged storms, they could be marooned on the rock for a week or more at a time. But the work continued more or less without a break for nearly fifteen months.

By January 1, 1881, the project was all but complete and the station's colossal Fresnel lens nearly ready for service. Ironically, that same evening a gale swept in out of the northwest, and a ship caught in the grip of the storm careened into the rock. The doomed vessel, a Japan-bound freighter known as the *Lupatia*, split apart and sank, carrying her entire crew to the bottom.

Admiralty Head Light, Washington

Had the *Lupatia* sailed only a few days later, the Tillamook Rock Light would have been in operation and might very well have saved her.

Unlike the beacon at Heceta Head, the Tillamook Rock Light no longer shines. The station was deactivated in 1951 after more than seventy-five years of service. Nowadays the rock and its old light station serve as a privately operated columbarium where families deposit the ashes of deceased loved ones.

At many points along the coast of the Pacific Northwest, lighthouse engineers and construction crews grappled with difficulties equal to or exceeding those facing them at Heceta Head.

Tillamook Rock is only one of countless stony outcroppings that make the nation's Pacific coast a deadly obstacle course for ships. Among the more threatening obstructions is ominously named Destruction Island located a few miles off the west coast of Washington State. During the early 1890s, government crews built a lighthouse here, a project that required more than three years of hard work. Some might say it took not three years, but more than thirty, to establish the Destruction Island Light. Congress first appropriated funding for the station way back in 1855, but for a variety of political and practical reasons, this money was never spent. The plan to mark the island with a first-rate navigational beacon was abandoned and forgotten for several decades until it was resurrected in the late 1880s.

Destruction Island Light, Washington

Work on the station's ninety-four-foot brick tower, residence, and other structures began in 1888, but progress was slow. Supplies and equipment delivered by lighthouse tenders had to be brought ashore on barges and then lifted to the top of the ninety-foot cliffs. Daily drenching rains made conditions miserable for construction crews while damaging storms and funding shortages brought unexpected delays. Finally, on New Year's Eve in 1891, keeper Christian Zauner was able to display the station's beacon.

Life at the Destruction Island Lighthouse was little more pleasant for its keepers than it had been for the workers who had built it. Constant rain, gray skies, and isolation made this station unpopular with keepers. One depressed coastguardsman assigned to Destruction Island described the place as "forlorn, dreary, and barren." No doubt, the station's keeper and assistants were happy to leave when the beacon was automated in 1963.

Another important navigational station established during the 1890s was the Umpqua River Lighthouse near Wincester Bay, Oregon. An earlier lighthouse built here in 1855 was undercut by erosion and collapsed into the river after only a few years of service. More than thirty years passed before Congress appropriated funds for a replacement. When construction of the new lighthouse began in 1892, engineers had to find a way to protect it from the river's marauding waters. They solved the problem through the rather

Umpqua River Light, Oregon

simple expedient of placing the sixty-five-foot tower and associated structures on an elevated site more than a hundred feet above the river. Completed in 1894, the station remains in use, as does its original first-order Fresnel lens.

Many of the northwest's most historic lighthouses do not face the open ocean, but rather mark the maze of straits and channels often referred to collectively as Puget Sound. Located a hundred miles or more from the Pacific, these sentinels guard the shipping lanes that link the Strait of Juan de Fuca with Seattle, Tacoma, and Olympia, Washington's capitol city.

Entering the Sound from the northwest, mariners are likely to spot the Point Wilson Light near Point Townsend. The beacon is focused by a classic fourth-order Fresnel lens housed in a small lantern room atop the station's forty-six-foot, octagonal concrete tower. Completed in 1914, this structure took the place of an earlier tower, which once stood on the roof of the two-story wooden keeper's residence.

Vessels moving southward from Port Townsend can rely on the guidance of the Point No Point Light. Although certainly no giant, this squat, thirty-foot tower stands tall in the eyes of mariners, who usually can see its flashing beacon from fifteen miles away. Established in 1879, the station remains in operation, making effective use of the same fourth-order lens installed here one-and-a-quarter centuries ago.

Point Robinson Light, Washington
Following pages: West Point Light, Washington

A near twin of the Point No Point Lighthouse can be found at West Point, now part of Seattle's Discovery Park. The West Point Lighthouse dates to 1881, when it was completed by the same construction crews that had recently built the Point No Point tower. The West Point tower still houses an operational fourth-order Fresnel lens, and is a favorite destination of park visitors.

Because of its proximity to Seattle and comfortable dwelling as well as the gentle beauty of the nearby land-scape, the West Point Lighthouse was a preferred duty station for keepers. Apparently, the same could be said of the classic, Victorian-style Mukilteo Lighthouse just north of Seattle. Peter Christianson, Mukilteo's first keeper, served here from the time the lighthouse was completed in 1906 until he died of natural causes in 1925. The last Mukilteo keeper retired in 1979 when the light was automated. Afterward, the Coast Guard intended to replace the station's old Fresnel lens with a modern optic, but this decision was reversed when nos-talgic locals complained.

Mukilteo Light, Washington
Following pages: Mukilteo
Light, Washington

CHAPTER SIX

Great Lake Lights— Legends and Lore

O ne of the most famous shipwrecks in history occurred on November 10, 1975, when the 729-foot freighter *Edmund Fitzgerald* broke apart and sank during a furious late-autumn blizzard. Interestingly, this calamity took place not on the high seas, but rather in the middle of a lake—Lake Superior. While wrecks on the Great Lakes are nothing unusual— in fact, they are quite common—this was an event of some magnitude. The *Fitzgerald* was once the biggest ship on the lakes. When she went down, she took Captain Ernest McSorley with her, along with his entire crew of twenty-eight experienced sailors and a mammoth 26,000-ton cargo of iron ore.

To those unfamiliar with the Great Lakes, it may come as a surprise that such a thing could happen on a lake, even one as big as the aptly named Superior. But these are neither small nor gentle bodies of water. Strewn with rocks and shoals and lashed by storms throughout the year, Lakes Superior, Michigan, Huron, Erie, and Ontario have swallowed up thousands of vessels, large and small, and countless thousands of mariners.

Whitefish Point Light, Michigan

Because the lakes are so heavily traveled and so vital to the economic well-being of both the United States and Canada, they have been marked from end to end with lighthouses. Michigan, with its 3,288 miles of lake shoreline, has more lighthouses than any other state. One of these, the Whitefish Point Lighthouse on Michigan's Upper Peninsula played an important role in the story and legend of the *Edmund Fitzgerald*.

Mariners and maritime officials long recognized the strategic importance of Whitefish Point, located at the end of a wedge-shaped peninsula partially separating the waters of Lake Superior from those of Whitefish Bay. Ships headed eastward toward the locks at Sault Ste. Marie invariably pass by Whitefish Point, and the captains of vessels caught in rough weather on the open lake eagerly watch for it since the relative calm of the bay waits just on the other side.

The government established a light station at Whitefish Point as early as 1848. Shortly before the Civil War, the original masonry tower was replaced by the seventy-six-foot iron-skeleton structure that remains in use today. Fitted with a third-order Fresnel lens—later exchanged for a powerful aero-marine optic—the station's beacon could reach fifteen to twenty miles out into the lake.

Strewn with rocks and shoals and lashed by storms throughout the year, Lakes Superior, Michigan, Huron, Erie, and Ontario have swallowed up thousands of vessels, large and small, and countless thousands of mariners.

Eagle Harbor Light, Michigan

No doubt, Captain McSorley was scanning the horizon looking for the Whitefish Point Light when the *Fitzgerald* met her end in November 1975. He never got close enough to make use of it for navigation, but he would not have seen it anyway. Ironically, on the fateful evening when he and his ship needed it most, the Whitefish Point Light was dark. Storm winds had knocked down the transmission lines that fed electric power to the station.

Such fascinating, tragic, and ironic tales have touched the shores of all the lakes. During the Revolutionary War, the British fighting ship *Ontario* set sail for Port Oswego on Lake Ontario with a detachment of the king's soldiers and an army payroll chest filled with gold and silver coins. Somewhere near Thirty Mile Point, about thirty miles east of the Niagara River mouth, the *Ontario* fell victim to one of the Great Lakes' notorious autumn storms. The *Ontario* ended up on the lake bottom along with the soldiers and the shipment of gold and silver.

In 1876, almost exactly one century after the *Ontario* sinking, a lighthouse was built on Thirty Mile Point. Its gray, limestone walls and red-and-white lantern became familiar sights to mariners moving along the southern side of the lake. It remains familiar today to fortune hunters who have never stopped searching for the *Ontario*'s treasure. The station's third-order light, taken out of service in 1959, was reactivated in 1998 as a private aid to navigation. Now part of Golden Hill State Park, the old keeper's dwelling houses a museum.

Thirty Mile Point Light,
New York

The most famous Great Lakes wartime event took place during the War of 1812 on Lake Erie, where Commodore Oliver Hazard Perry, then a mere lieutenant, handed the British Great Lakes fleet a resounding defeat. The message Perry sent ashore when the fighting was over— "We have met the enemy and they are ours"— rallied public morale and helped the United States keep possession of its Great Lakes territories. Only eight years after the battle and just a few miles from the place where it was fought, masons constructed what is now one of the oldest U.S. government buildings on the lakes—the Marblehead Lighthouse.

Maritime officials understood that the battles fought by most mariners in Lake Erie were against darkness, hidden shoals, and high waves whipped up by sudden storms. To help lake sailors cope and find safe harbor, Congress funded construction of a sixty-five-foot limestone tower at Marblehead, a few miles north of Sandusky, Ohio. For decades, the station was equipped with old style lamps and reflectors, but in 1858, this inferior optical system was exchanged for a fine third-order Fresnel lens. Nowadays, a modern plastic lens serves here, but the old Fresnel, now on display in a nearby museum, guided vessels for at least a century.

The Marblehead Fresnel had been in use for only a few years when the Civil War broke out and nearby Johnston Island was made a prisoner-of-war camp for captured Confederate soldiers. For many of the homesick southerners, the station's bright beacon came to symbolize

Marblehead Light, Ohio

their plight. In the letters they wrote to their loved ones in the South, they often mentioned the light and said it seemed to be calling them home. Some believe the ghosts of southern prisoners who died on the island still walk its shores.

A modern-day ghost is said to darken the staircases—and brighten the lens—of the Old Presque Isle Lighthouse on Michigan's Lake Huron shore. The rather roughly constructed thirty-eight-foot brick and stone tower is referred to as "old" because it was built in 1840 and has not seen regular use since 1871, when a "new" 113-foot structure took over its task of guiding Lake Huron shipping. The New Presque Isle Lighthouse remains an active aid to navigation, focusing its beacon with a third-order Fresnel lens.

Sold to private owners more than a century ago, the Old Presque Isle Lighthouse eventually became a maritime museum operated by the local township. Although there is a small lens in the lantern room, it is never used. Even so, boaters on the lake sometimes say they can see a light in the old tower. Museum visitors have reported speaking to a mysterious "keeper" in the lantern room.

If any lighthouse is haunted, it ought to be the one at Round Island near the famed Straits of Mackinac linking Lakes Michigan and Huron. Built in 1895, then deactivated and abandoned shortly after World War II, the Round Island Lighthouse deteriorated to the point of collapse before local preservationists stepped in to

New Presque Isle Light, Michigan
Following pages: Round Island Light, Michigan

save it. The two-story brick tower and attached keeper's residence had begun to fall apart by 1982, when it was featured in the movie "Somewhere in Time." In the film, a man (played by Christopher Reeve), reaches back in time to reestablish his relationship with a ghostly, early 1900s lover.

Perhaps it is not too much to say that the Friends of the Round Island Lighthouse and Great Lake Lighthouse Keepers Association rescued an important part of their own—and the nation's—past by pitching in to save this historic light station. Now handsomely restored and protected from the lake's encroaching waters, the red-and-white Round Island Lighthouse can be seen from the decks of ferries approaching Mackinac Island, the popular tourist retreat.

> Because the lakes are so heavily traveled and so vital to the economic well-being of both the United States and Canada, they have been marked from end to end with lighthouses.

The Great Lakes can claim more than their share of ghost ships—vessels such as the *Edmund Fitzgerald* that vanished, often in mysterious circumstances. In fact, the very first European-style vessel to ply the fresh waters of the Great Lakes never completed her first roundtrip voyage. During the late 1670s, the French adventurer La Salle built the sixty-foot *Griffin*, arming her with cannon and sailing her deep into the Great Lakes region, perhaps as far as the western shores of Lake Michigan. Having loaded the *Griffin* with a rich cargo of beaver pelts, he sent the ship back

Seul Choix Pointe Light,
Michigan
Following pages:
St. Joseph North Pierhead
Lights, Michigan

toward the French trading colonies in the east. The *Griffin* never reached her destination, and to this day, no one knows for sure what became of her.

It is all too obvious what happened to the *Carl C. Bradley*, a 640-foot freighter destroyed by a raging Lake Michigan gale in November 1858—coincidentally, the same year the *Edmund Fitzgerald* was first launched. Her hull bashed in by huge waves, the *Bradley* simply split apart and sank, carrying all but two of her thirty-five officers and crew to the bottom. To help other vessels avoid a similar fate, the lake's shores have been lined with lighthouses.

Some of Lake Michigan's prominent navigational beacons shine from tall towers such as the 107-foot, iron-plated brick cylinder at Big Sable Point (built in 1867) in Michigan, the soaring 108-foot brick tower at Wind Point (1880), Wisconsin, or the 87-foot brick sentinel at Seul Choix (1895) on Michigan's Upper Peninsula. Many other important light towers are located on stone or concrete piers reaching half a mile or more into the lake.

A particularly fine example of a pier lighthouse can be found at St. Joseph, Michigan, where two separate towers with their own distinct beacons guide vessels into harbor. Built during the early twentieth century, the towers stand several hundred feet apart and are connected by an elevated catwalk. This arrangement allows the beacons to function as "range lights," and navigators

Sand Island Light,
Wisconsin

approaching the harbor try to keep them lined up one behind the other. The St. Joseph Station puts on a brilliant light show in the evening when its beacons are in operation and the catwalk is lit up. The station is so handsome, both at night and during the day, that it has been featured on a postage stamp.

But perhaps the Great Lakes' most beautiful lighthouse is the one that crowns Split Rock in Minnesota, near the far western end of Lake Superior. Poised at the edge of a 120-foot granite cliff, the yellow-brick, octagonal Split Rock tower was built by immigrant laborers in 1910. The tower and its third-order lens were intended to help ore freighters and other vessels keep safely within the shipping channels that skirt the lake's northwestern shores. The station's big Fresnel lens was of a type known as a clamshell, which funneled light into a single powerful flash.

> [F]ascinating, tragic, and ironic tales have touched the shores of all the lakes.

Deactivated in 1969, the Split Rock Lighthouse no longer guides mariners. Instead, it serves as a museum and historic attraction celebrating the maritime heritage of the Great Lakes, the nation, and the world. Visitors learn much about the old-fashioned but nonetheless effective technology that enabled lighthouse keepers to save ships and lives. Of course, there are some vessels that could never be saved by any lighthouse, no matter how bright its beacon. One of these was the *Edmund Fitzgerald*. Each year on the evening of November 10,

Split Rock Light, Minnesota

the anniversary of the *Fitzgerald* disaster, the Split Rock beacon is relit for a few hours in memory of the big freighter and her doomed crew and of the countless thousands of other ships and mariners lost throughout the ages.

Like the deactivated Split Rock and Old Point Loma Lights, many of America's lighthouses now serve primarily as historical attractions or museums. Many other old towers, like the much-celebrated giant at Cape Hatteras, the two-century-old tower at Portland Head, the red-brick architectural wonder at Ponce de Leon Inlet, and the cliff-top sentinel at Heceta Head, continue to guide mariners as active aids to navigation. But all of America's lighthouses remain an invaluable link to the past. No less than Independence Hall or the Washington Memorial, these venerable structures are historic treasures, invaluable reminders of rich maritime heritage we cannot afford to disregard.

Wind Point Light,
Wisconsin

INDEX

CREDITS

All photographs are © Bruce Roberts except the following: "Map of Rhode Island and Long Island from Narragansett Bay to Peconic Bay (1779)" (background on box): courtesy of the Library of Congress; Heceta Head Light (front cover and p. 97): © Stuart Westmorland/CORBIS; Sandy Hook Light (p. 24) © William G. Kaufhold; Alcatraz Island Light (pp. 76–77): courtesy of Bob and Sandra Shanklin; Cape Disappointment Light (p. 79): © Philip James Corwin/CORBIS; Cape Flattery Light (p. 80): © Richard A. Cooke/CORBIS; Point Bonita Light (pp. 92–93): © Richard Cummins/CORBIS; Destruction Island Light (p. 105): courtesy of Bob and Sandra Shanklin; West Point Light (p. 110): Todd Bates.